mag.nan.i.mous

BE THE ONE
EVERYONE WANTS
TO DO BUSINESS WITH

mag.nan.i.mous

BE THE ONE
EVERYONE WANTS
TO DO BUSINESS WITH

DAYNA MASON

Printed in the United States of America

First Printing: December 2023

ISBN 979-8-87-017992-6

(Softcover)

Visit the author's website at www.daynajo.com

Dedicated to my
magnanimous grandchildren:

Olliver, Winter, and Lillian

CONTENTS

mag.nan.i.mous

BE THE ONE
EVERYONE WANTS
TO DO BUSINESS WITH

introduction

"I hate the whole self-help industry ..." begins a YouTube video featuring Simon Sinek, the author of the business book *Start With Why*. "How can *you* be happy?" he continues. "What are the five steps *you* can follow to be a millionaire? What are seven steps that *you* need to get the career that *you* want? You know, me, me, me, me, me, me, me, me, me."

Chances are you picked up this book with the same motivation that's in all of us: "What's in it for me?" There's nothing wrong with that. In fact, it's hard-wired into us for survival. But there's a difference between surviving and thriving.

Did you know that the only way to feel fulfilled (to thrive) is to focus on others? When we're fulfilled, the ups and downs of life are experienced more like waves than tsunamis and life's disruptions rarely impact our overall satisfaction with life.

So, what does this have to do with being "magnanimous" and "the one everyone wants to do business with?" You know what happens when you take an interest in others? They want to do business with you. Not because you're offering the best product or service, but because they like you.

Sure, we could use one of the many "strategies" to manipulate them to do business with us—"low, low, low, price," "our product is the best," "our service is the best," etc. There's a big difference between a transaction and loyalty. Loyal people are willing to turn down a better product, price, or service to continue doing business with us and often don't research the competition or entertain other options.

We can influence people one of two ways: by manipulating them or inspiring them.

Do you want to be on the constant hunt for the latest manipulations (aka "strategies") to get new business to replace the old business that went elsewhere? Or would you rather enjoy getting to know people in a way that ultimately leads them to do business with you for as long as they need what you have to offer?

There are plenty of resources available that tell you how to convince people to do business with you. But, if you want to inspire people rather than manipulate them and feel fulfilled in the process, let's get started learning how to establish relationships with others that will result in attracting all the business you could ever want.

about this book

This book takes a holistic approach to the topic of magnanimity, covering both the personal and professional growth perspectives.

While this book is focused on becoming irresistible to attract more business, it's important to understand that *who we are* permeates *all* aspects of our lives. For example, if we carefully select the perfect gift for someone, it doesn't matter whether they are a friend or a client. The act of giving the gift will feel the same. Because we can't compartmentalize actions from the heart. There isn't a business heart and a personal heart. Likewise, when we operate from our heart, not only will we attract clients, we'll also be attractive to those in our personal lives.

After over thirty years as a successful entrepreneur, through trial and error, combined with a lifelong interest in what makes people tick, I've come to understand some fundamentals for business success. This knowledge allows me to pursue the business life that I *want* (even when sometimes it doesn't seem logical) and realize success and happiness doing it. I hope sharing this information will help readers make business decisions that lead to more business, *and* greater happiness in all areas of life.

#1

what does it mean to be magnanimous?

The word magnanimous comes from the Latin, magnus, meaning "great" and animus, meaning "spirit" or "heart."

Someone who is magnanimous has a *great heart*.

We are born with built-in empathy and goodness.

Before babies can even speak, they are capable of distinguishing right from wrong and making moral decisions, according to a series of studies at Yale University's Infant Cognition Center, also known as "The Baby Lab." [1]

The puppet experiments

Researchers present a puppet show to babies, where one puppet tries to push a ball up a hill. Then, either another puppet comes along and helps the first puppet push the ball up the hill, or another puppet shows up and hinders the first puppet by pushing the ball down the hill.

After the babies watch these scenarios, the researchers present both the helpful and unhelpful puppets to the babies to see which puppet the three-to ten-month-old babies reach for. Almost every baby reaches for the helping puppet. Even more amazing is that babies as young as twelve weeks old also choose the helpful puppet. While young babies can't reach yet, they can control their eyes and science indicates that they look at what they like. When presented with the two puppets, most of the young babies look at and settle their gaze toward the nice puppets.

The puppet experiments prove that babies have a general appreciation of good and bad behavior, and they show a basic disposition of goodness.

We innately appreciate the good in others and we never outgrow it.

The way we conduct ourselves in our personal lives matters to our business lives. If we treat our clients well, but we are rude to the server at a restaurant, it's noticed. We don't know who's watching or where our next business relationship is going to come from. When we stay consistently respectful and kind in the way we treat others, always, we don't have to worry about our business relationships.

Being magnanimous means using the generous and kindhearted nature we were born with to seek understanding and extend tolerance. Magnanimity is the virtue of being great of mind and heart. It encompasses a refusal to be petty, and a willingness to take risks and actions for noble (high moral) purposes. When we demonstrate magnanimity, others may find us irresistible.

What makes magnanimous people so irresistible?

Magnanimous people radiate generosity—*greatheartedness.*

They treat everyone they encounter with respect. Not because anyone has earned their respect, but because magnanimous people are respectful. As my good friend Diane Pechacek says, "No one has to earn my respect. I respect because I'm a respectful person. People have to earn my admiration. But respect flows out of who I am."

Magnanimous people recognize that dignity is the right of a person to be valued and respected for their own sake, and to be treated ethically.

We all judge. Judgment is essential for good decision-making. But when we silently or openly criticize someone based on nothing but our perception, we get a glimpse of our own limitations or perceived weaknesses. In other words, our motivation for criticizing others is often rooted in our desire to feel better about ourselves. For example, when we complain about someone's behavior, we may think, I would never do that. But beneath this comparison to demonstrate our superiority, we may be avoiding our feelings of failure with discipline in an area of our own lives. When we're feeling insecure or scared, we're even more likely to assign negative meaning to others' actions to help us feel better.

Judging someone doesn't define who they are; it defines who we are.

Deep down most of us know that judging others isn't a good practice and we don't trust or enjoy being around people who do it frequently. We understand that it's impossible to know the full story behind what motivates another person. We also know what it feels like to be misunderstood. It's just as easy to assume the best about people as to assume the worst, and feels better too. The more compassion we have for others, the more compassion we'll have for ourselves. When we make sure that our behavior lines up with what we value and show kindness, compassion, and respect towards others, we can be quite irresistible.

Magnanimous people love life and see obstacles as temporary setbacks. Their positive attitude makes others want to be a part of whatever they've got going on and they're great at making others feel comfortable. They know that not everyone wants to be treated the same. For example, some people love public recognition and others would rather hide in a corner than draw attention to themselves.

Magnanimous people are observant, seek to understand others, and are genuinely interested in learning more about the people they interact with. They listen to understand rather than listen to respond, asking open-ended follow-up questions. They put their phone away and give others their undivided attention. They make others feel *seen*.

When we take a genuine interest in people, they feel a connection to us—like that of a trusted friend.

Benefits of being other-oriented

When we're self-oriented, we move about the world without paying much attention to the thoughts, needs and feelings of others. Over time, this orientation may prevent us from forming meaningful relationships and from realizing our full potential.

In contrast, prosocial behavior—the intent to benefit others—not only makes us feel good, but *we* experience more health and happiness advantages from being the *giver* than from being the recipient.

Being other-oriented is the conscious effort to put the thoughts, needs, and feelings of others first, without abandoning our own needs.

In a study at the National Institutes of Health, researchers discovered that we release feel-good and human-bonding chemicals (serotonin, dopamine and oxytocin) during gift-giving behaviors. Altruistic behavior also stimulates the reward center in the brain, causing a powerful physical sensation of euphoria. This is known as the "helper's high"— our built-in reward system for helping others.

Giving *feels really good.*

The results of another study (<u>Brown 2003</u>) indicate that mortality is significantly reduced for those who provide support to others, while receiving support had no effect on mortality. [2]

Giving *extends our life.*

Other-focused attention—compassion—triggers a decrease in heart rate (Calvo and Peters 2014). [3]

Giving *lessens our stress.*

When we go through hardships, performing simple acts of kindness can reduce our stress. In addition, studies have shown that when battling big problems like addiction, chronic pain, etc., our suffering is reduced when we connect with someone who is going through or has been through a similar situation. And when we are the *helper* we are twice as likely to alleviate our own similar struggle by helping another. This is known as the "Wounded Healer" principle.

Giving *makes burdens lighter.*

Numerous studies have found additional benefits that come from being other-oriented, including experiencing less anxiety, less trouble sleeping, a lower risk of depression and dementia, better heart health, better overall physical health, lower blood pressure, better friendships, and greater self-esteem and satisfaction with life.

Giving *makes us healthier and happier.*

Being other-oriented in business

Effective interpersonal skills—communication, listening and attitude—are critical to a thriving business and can make or break our career and our company's success. When we combine these skills with an altruistic focus on our client, the results can set us apart from the competition in ways we haven't imagined.

Businesses that promote an other-oriented culture reap greater rewards than their competitors in the areas of performance improvement, team building, leadership development, conflict management, job satisfaction, customer satisfaction, and ultimately, financial gain.

Ross Shafer's story

In the late 1980s, my friend Ross Shafer hosted *The Late Show,* a nightly talk show on FOX. He wanted Elizabeth Taylor to be a guest in hopes that she would enjoy the experience so much that she would encourage her important celebrity friends to agree to be guests. Unfortunately, she was unavailable, so in her place she sent her boyfriend at the time, Malcolm Forbes, the head of the Forbes business empire.

Ross had been trained for this. It was "Talk Show 101." Never talk about yourself, show extreme interest, lean in, and ask follow-up questions. He wanted to make sure that Malcolm had a great time, so he'd tell his friends, leading to other big-name guests.

The interview lasted only 5.5 minutes.

After the show, Ross said to Malcolm, "I had a great time and I hope you did too."

Malcolm replied, "You're a fascinating young man. Would you like to go hot-air ballooning with Liz and I this weekend?"

Ross thought to himself, *Fascinating young man? He knows nothing about me.*

He accepted Malcolm's invitation. In the basket of the hot-air balloon, Ross looked around at Malcolm and his friends and thought, *This is impossible. How did I get into the billionaire boys club?*

Ross was professionally curious and trained *not* to talk about himself. Malcolm knew nothing about Ross, yet he thought of him as *fascinating* and wanted to spend more time with him. Why?

Because he couldn't wait to hear more about *himself.*

Studies repeatedly show that our favorite topic to talk about is *ourselves.* Science has determined that when we talk about ourselves, the brain "lights up" in the same way as when we eat good food or engage in sex. It's gratifying and feels good.

If we encourage someone to talk about themselves, they will feel so good, they will think *we* are fascinating.

Years later, while reflecting on his experience with Malcolm Forbes, Ross realized there was a need in the business world for the same other-oriented training he'd acquired as a talk show host. In 2018 Ross and his business partner Garry Poole founded the training program, Other-Focused™ Living an Other Focused Life.

Ross believes, "When we're self-absorbed, we have zero scalability. Conversely, when we focus on others, our lives become scalable—capable of expansive progress while elegantly managing the growth—and others become our champions, spreading the word about us."

Magnanimous people are other-oriented.

When we are other-oriented, not only will others become our champions; our kindness will inspire altruistic behavior in others.

Domino effect of giving

When one person behaves generously it inspires observers to do the same, according to research conducted at University of California. The study found that witnessing one act of kindness prompts observers to pay it forward, and those individuals' kindness triggers more observers to be kind, etc. One person can potentially influence hundreds of others with one simple generous gesture.

In the Other-Focused™ program they found that "People who live other-focused lives, and practice putting others first, realize the powerful, positive impact they make in the world around them. Why? What do they see? They see people who smile more because they feel sincerely cared for and valued. They see people who shed a tear of joy because they feel heard and understood, maybe for the first time in a long time. They see people who sit up straight and glow brighter because they feel celebrated. They see people who rise to the occasion and accomplish more than they ever dreamed because they feel validated and championed. They see people who also want to live other-focused lives now because they've experienced first-hand how it feels to be treated like they matter."

Science supports the idea that being other-oriented helps us in all areas of our lives—business, personal, health, and wellbeing. When we give to others, we not only feel the "helper's high," we experience wellness, longevity, fulfillment, and a sense of purpose. We *receive* more benefits from our giving than our recipient does from our gift.

> *"For it is in giving that we receive."*
> - Saint Francis of Assisi

The more we focus on others, the more irresistible we'll be.

Heart-driven business relationships

In our jargon-rich business environments, we talk about things like; What does she "bring to the table"? ... We need to get his "buy-in" ... What we really need is more "facetime" ... or ... We need to "circle back." Contrived, impersonal, meaningless rhetoric.

If we spent less time coming up with cool buzzwords to describe our poor attempts at relationships with our clients and spent more time just building a relationship with them, we wouldn't have a need for the implementation of a "winning sales strategy."

Have you ever been in the middle of explaining something important to someone, and they started checking their phone for messages? Or maybe they just got that glazed-over look like they were going through a "to do" list in their head. How did that make you feel? Did you even care anymore about what it was you were trying to explain? Chances are you felt they simply didn't care what you had to say, or more specifically, *they didn't care about you.*

Would you want to do business with someone who at best is not paying attention and at worst simply doesn't care?

How does it feel to have someone genuinely listen to you? Not just listen because they need something from you— information, performance improvement, an explanation— but sincerely listen, because they care about you? This is the stuff that relationship is made of. When you believe someone cares about you, not just because of what you can do for them, but because they honestly value you as a person—don't you want to do things for them, help them, and contribute to their success?

When your heart is in it—when you care about the people *more* than the business "bottom line"—that is when it becomes possible to achieve those ridiculously remarkable results for your Profit and Loss Statement that defy reason. And caring doesn't mean letting people do whatever they want, whenever they want. Similar to your relationship with your children, sometimes it's necessary to hold them accountable for their actions and sometimes even kick them out of the nest. But all your actions, when heart-driven, are what *is* best for that person you care about and ultimately for your business.

Magnanimous people are heart-driven.

How to have more productive conversations

Much of what passes for conversation today is simply monologue. We may take turns talking, but no one is actually listening. I say what I want to say and while you're talking, instead of seeking to understand, I'm thinking about what I want to say next. Productive conversation requires dialogue—the process of understanding and reasoning.

When we're *telling*, we're not *listening*. If all we do is *tell*, we learn nothing. Conversations that inspire and transform require curiosity and respect.

Promote beneficial dialogue

Social media has made it easier than ever to be disrespectful and say things we wouldn't say if we were face to face. It's easy to tell someone they are an idiot if there's no risk of them punching you in the face. But these interactions lead to nothing beneficial for anyone.

Thoughtful, reflective, mature, and reasoned dialogue is necessary for constructive discussion. Dialogue requires curiosity. If we aren't open to changing our viewpoint, conversation not only loses its value but our disagreement can devolve into insults.

To promote dialogue that's beneficial, we need to soften our stance. Let go of our need to be right. Listen to understand the other's viewpoint. Listen as if we actually care about their thoughts.

When confronted with information that contradicts our perspective, we can accept that we may not know everything, or may even be wrong. If our emotions are triggered, it is almost impossible to have a valuable discussion. It's better to take a step back and wait until we feel calm again before reengaging in conversation. When we're calm we can examine our assumptions and create communication that encourages mutual discovery.

Conversation that is both inspirational and valuable begins with "humane communication."

"Humane communication" and productive conversation

The early definition of the word "humane" meant "courteous, friendly, civil, obliging." This definition evolved over time to include "marked by tenderness, compassion, and a disposition to kindly treat others."

Practicing *humane communication* can greatly improve our interactions with others.

Rather than assume that people who disagree with us are bad or ignorant, we can assume good intentions and imagine that in their own way, they want what is best even if their views are difficult to understand. For example, someone may state that religion is harmful and to be avoided. Instead of preparing an argument for why they are wrong, we could seek to understand why they hold that belief. We may discover that they had a traumatic church experience. We still may not agree with their conclusion, but now we understand that their belief is based on a desire to prevent others from experiencing the same pain they did.

We don't have to agree with others, but we can show respect, which includes due regard for their feelings, wishes, rights, and traditions. Try to see another person's view from their perspective and experience and be willing to learn from them. When we understand why someone believes as they do, it's easier to have empathy for their beliefs even when we disagree.

We can take the time to understand both sides of the debate. It's difficult to persuade someone to see your point of view if you don't understand theirs. At the center of meaningful conversation is our willingness to not only appreciate the right of others to disagree with us but to see it as an opportunity to learn something new.

We can filter our thoughts. Not everything we think needs to be communicated. If what we are thinking is not helpful to the conversation, we can keep it to ourselves.

Productive conversations are the result of humane communication—the genuine exchange of thoughts, beliefs and ideas through non-defensive dialogue which helps us develop wisdom and can result in powerful insights that lead to worthwhile agreements.

When we take humane communication into a business setting, we're able to see beyond what our client says they want or need to what they didn't even know they wanted. Henry Ford, the founder of the Ford Motor Company, said, "If I'd asked people what they wanted, they would have said a faster horse." People at that time didn't know that driving a car was even possible, but Henry Ford did, and he knew what his customers wanted beyond what they thought they wanted.

When we listen to understand, we're able to give our clients things they never would've thought to ask for.

Everyone wants to be seen and heard

Everyone you meet just wants to be seen and heard. The South African Zulu greeting, "Sawubona," was made popular by the movie *Avatar*. In the movie, the characters greet each other by saying, "I see you," the English translation of sawubona. As the movie explains, this means more than seeing the other physically with your eyes. It means seeing into the other, understanding the other, embracing the other—seeing the other person's heart. Sawubona is more than just a greeting. It recognizes the worth and dignity of each person. It says, "I see the whole of you—your experiences, your passions, your pain, your strengths and weaknesses, and your future. You are valuable to me." This greeting is infused with the belief that when others *see* me, then I exist.

When we give our full attention and presence to another, we communicate their value. When they feel *seen*, they become imbued with vitality—they come to life.

In our busy lives, we rarely feel *seen* by others. So, when someone truly notices us, gives us their undistracted attention, listens attentively, and asks questions ... we feel valued. We feel *seen*.

Magnanimous people make others feel seen.

"People will forget what you said, people will forget what you did, but people will never forget how you made them feel." - Maya Angelou

In business, if we give our clients and potential clients our undivided attention, make the effort to *see* them, we foster trust that leads to long-term business loyalty.

Radical consideration

Sometimes we overestimate our impact on others. Sometimes we underestimate it. Sometimes we don't estimate it at all. Our view of the world is from the perspective of "me" and we *often* miscalculate how our words and actions affect others. But our influence is far more powerful than we may realize.

Our choices impact others whether we know it or not

In an Instagram post, my friend, Sean Brown (@seans_thoughts), pondered his drive home, during which he saw someone walking on the side of the road. He didn't notice the man at first. Sean wrote, "The guy was doing nothing wrong. The problem was, in his dark clothing, he was invisible." Sean thought, "What if I was distracted? What if I hit him?"

Sean's post caused me to consider the situation from a whole new perspective. When the walker dressed that day, he didn't think about the impact his choices might have on someone else. If he thought at all about dressing for visibility, it would likely have been so he *wouldn't get hit by a car*. But what if he'd practiced what I call "radical consideration" and thought about the potential impact *to the driver of the car*? With this new perspective—a more complete picture of both the danger to himself and the potential devastation to the driver—the walker may have made a different clothing choice—an action that might not only save his own life, but prevent shattering the driver's life.

When we act based solely on our view of how our actions impact *ourselves*—an incomplete perspective—we miss opportunities to impact the world the way we truly intend.

Practice radical consideration to get what we intend

We have a much greater influence on those around us than we realize. If we take the time to practice radical consideration, we'll have a better chance of getting our intended results in life.

The word "radical" means "far-reaching or thorough." The word "consideration" means "thoughtfulness and sensitivity toward others." When we practice *radical consideration*, we carefully consider another person's point of view and our impact on them. This thoughtfulness exposes our blind spots and leads to altruistic actions that help others and make us feel good.

A Starbucks barista in Leesburg, Virginia, understands radical consideration. One of her regular customers was deaf, so he would place his order by typing it on his phone and showing it to her. One day she surprised him by asking for his order in American Sign Language. She then handed him a note that said, "I've been learning American Sign Language so you can have the same experience as everyone else." He was so touched by the gesture that he posted about it on Facebook, and the post quickly went viral.

Magnanimous people practice radical consideration. They know that our influence is more powerful than we realize.

Two of the scariest things we do are: ask for something, and say "no"

A series of studies conducted on subways in New York City in 1978 by the famous researcher, Dr. Stanley Milgram, found that most people would rather give up their seat on a train than say "no." The experimenters were asked to repeatedly board a crowded train, ask someone for their seat and note the number of times their request was honored. Surprisingly, 68% of those asked gave up their seat. But what researchers found even more surprising was that the majority of experimenters not only expected everyone to say "no," they were terrified of asking.

We're often afraid of making a request of someone, not realizing that they are equally afraid of saying no to our request.

Our "egocentric bias" causes us to misjudge how different other people's viewpoints are from our own or causes us to ignore their viewpoints completely. We assume everyone thinks and acts like we do, so we don't even consider what their perspective might actually be.

In the case of the Milgram subway experiment, the participants' bias caused them to underestimate the power of asking for what they wanted. When we ask someone for something, they may feel pressure to say yes, but research indicates that after they honor our request, they often feel good about their altruistic behavior.

In another, more famous Milgram experiment, subjects were asked to administer electric shocks to participants who answered questions incorrectly. Most of the subjects were willing to apply what they believed were lethal shocks to participants simply because they were told to do so. They didn't want to say "no." This is an extreme example of the importance of being able to say *no* when we need to.

Ask, say no, and consider our impact

We can influence our world more intentionally with three simple practices: ask for what we want, say no to what we don't want, and radically consider the impact of what we say and do.

Our fear of rejection can cause us to avoid asking for what we want, but the truth is that approximately seven out of ten times we will get a "yes."

Saying no is difficult for everyone, and most people expect a "no" to their requests anyway. So, saying no when we need to becomes both exceptional and potentially life-changing.

Monty Roberts, the famous California horse trainer, and author of the bestselling book, *The Man Who Listens to Horses,* changed the trajectory of his life with a *no* early in his career.

He was training as an apprentice under one of the best trainers in the business, Don Dodge. Monty had only four horses in his care, and he was barely making enough money to support his family. When Monty's 10-week apprenticeship ended, Dodge told him to contact the owner of one of the horses he was training and tell him that he was wasting his money because that horse was never going to amount to anything. Monty knew this would eliminate a fourth of his meager earnings, but he made the call.

The owner was furious and told Monty he would never give him another horse to train. Several days later, news of Monty's action spread amongst other horse owners, who already knew the truth about the horse's lack of ability. They were impressed by Monty's honesty even though he would lose money.

Because of his *no*, Monty gained a reputation as a great and honest trainer, and he soon had plenty of horses to train, including training horses for the Queen of England.

We often underestimate the influence of our choices.

Magnanimous people know the power of courageously asking, bravely saying no, and going beyond our personal viewpoint to radically consider others. They understand this approach will invite more of what we need to attract all the business we could ever want and live a happier and more meaningful life in the process.

#2

build trust, be honest

Lying is a slippery slope and damages trust. When we're dedicated to honesty, we promote meaningful relationships, client loyalty, and become all that lying helps us pretend we already are.

Why we lie

We all lie. Yet most of us also consider ourselves honest. We justify our lies by telling ourselves the lie was necessary to protect someone—even ourselves—to avoid pain, embarrassment, conflict, or hurt feelings. It might be to protect others perceptions of us. We want others to think well of us, so rather than admit our mistakes we cover them up.

Most of the time we get away with these little lies, so we continue thinking of them as useful tools. But even a small lie could expose us as a liar, which would damage our reputation and others' ability to trust us. One lie often leads to another, leading to even greater negative consequences if discovered. Meanwhile, the fear of discovery causes us more distress.

The truth may hurt but it doesn't harm

The truth might "hurt" briefly but deception "harms" us. For example, a friend invites us to an event that we don't want to attend. If we're honest and say we're not interested, we may hurt their feelings in that moment. But, if we lie and say we're busy and they discover our deception, we have not only hurt their feelings, we have betrayed their trust and harmed the relationship.

"Better to get hurt by the truth than comforted with a lie."—Khaled Hosseini, *The Kite Runner*

Profanity and honesty

A study published in *Social Psychological and Personality Science* (2017) found that "profanity was associated with less lying and deception at the individual level, and with higher integrity at the society level." [4]

"Profanity is the spontaneous expression of emotions such as anger, frustration, or surprise. The use of profanity is usually the unfiltered genuine expression of emotions, with the most extreme example the bursts of profanity accompanying Tourette syndrome. Speech involving profane words has a stronger impact on people than regular speech and has been shown to be processed on a deeper level in people's minds." (Jay, Caldwell-Harris, & King, 2008) [5]

People who swear are generally more honest. I'm not suggesting that we start swearing at our clients, but having this information, may help us recognize the authenticity behind profanity when we encounter it and be less offended.

We are human lie detectors

When we lie, we feel discomfort in our body, because our commitment to the lie is in opposition to who we really are. When we feel compelled to lie, our character defects are exposed, and we have an opportunity to examine them and make changes. When someone lies to us, we also feel a sensation of discomfort even if we don't consciously understand why.

I recently reflected on an event in my life where I felt misunderstood. Upon closer examination I realized that I wasn't actually misunderstood. Rather, I had unintentionally communicated an underlying truth that I was trying to hide with my choice of words.

While working on a craft project with some people in my community, someone placed inexpensive curling ribbon on top of expensive ribbon and I thought it looked "tacky." Not wanting to hurt anyone's feelings, I kept my thoughts to myself. Instead, I focused on my other truth and questioned their design choice based on expense. I asked, "Why cover up expensive ribbon with inexpensive curling ribbon?" and suggested sticking to one style to save money.

I believed my question was valid and justified, but what I didn't realize is that people are human lie detectors. Even though I never said the word "tacky," my underlying judgment was communicated anyway, and someone's feelings were hurt.

Although we cannot consciously discern when someone is lying, we do sense it on a less-conscious level. Often we then talk ourselves out of it. Research published in *Psychological Science* found that we all have pre-set instincts for detecting lies, but they are often overridden by our conscious minds. [6]

I recently worked with a client who backed out of a contract. They gave me a reason, but I could sense they were lying. My suspicions were later confirmed when they asked to work with me again and inadvertently disclosed the real reason they backed out of the first contract.

They didn't seem aware that their lie had been exposed, but it didn't matter. The damage was done—I no longer trusted them. If they'd told me the real reason to begin with, it still would've been a challenging situation, but we could've addressed it and handled it differently going forward.

Trying to hide our truth or pretending—attempting to present ourselves in a manner contrary to how we genuinely feel—simply doesn't work. It damages relationships and ultimately stunts our personal and business growth.

Benefits of honesty

Some people feel that they'll be rejected if they're honest, but the reality is that those who reject us for being honest don't care about us anyway. All you risk losing by being honest is the *illusion* of someone's affection or admiration. Conversely, lying can cause those who *do* care about us to reject us due to the betrayal they feel.

In business, lying damages trust. Deceiving our clients regardless of the reason eventually catches up with us and not only harms the relationship but can have a far-reaching impact on our business in general. Social media has made it easier than ever to amplify the wrong doings of any business and share those complaints with the public.

Deception doesn't have to be as obvious as a lie. Intentionally withholding information from our clients can have the same impact upon trust as a direct lie.

If lying doesn't truly protect anyone but can actually harm the relationships we care about, and those who are lied to can sense the lie anyway, why not strive for honesty?

When we develop a reputation for tactful but complete honesty and transparency, others know they can rely on us to tell the truth. Especially when it matters (even if it means turning away business). This reputation will not only solidify the loyalty of our current clients, it will attract new customers that *we want to work with*. Because if a new client is not a good fit for our product or service at this time, our honesty will ensure they will consider using us in the future when it does fit—*and* they will tell all their friends about the trustworthy experience.

Honesty builds trust. Trust builds loyalty.

Manipulation is a form of deception. Persuading clients to buy products and services they don't need or want, not only doesn't feel good, it prevents long-term business relationships.

Apple trains its retail employees to ask their customers questions in order to understand the problem they're trying to solve. Trainees are encouraged to direct customers to the best solution even if that solution doesn't result in an Apple purchase. For Apple, "customer experience" is prioritized over profit. Their philosophy is simply to make the customer happy. This seems to be a successful philosophy given Apple is currently valued at $2.95 trillion.

Magnanimous people value honesty.

#3

connecting
with others

To build long-lasting business relationships, we need to connect with our clients in a way that contributes positively to their lives. When we add value it's better for our client and the world. Giving of our time and attention can inspire a domino effect of generous behavior.

Make others feel important

Every person we encounter wants to know, "Do you see me? Do you hear me?"

Whether it's a friend or potential client, when we listen intently to someone—get genuinely curious about them, asking questions with no other agenda but to learn and understand, we connect with them in a way that goes far beyond any sales pitch we could ever concoct. We make them feel important, and when we make someone feel important, we become important to them. This connection establishes relationships with others, which means when the need arises for our product or service, *they* will reach out to *us*.

The first step when trying to connect with a client is to make them feel comfortable with you. The quickest way to put someone at ease is to make eye contact and smile at them.

The second step is to know what our first short, simple, open-ended, question will be. This question is the most important because when well chosen, it sets the stage for organic follow-up questions that help us to understand our client's needs on a deeper level. We don't want to ask yes or no questions or questions that allow for a quick answer. Instead, we want to ask open-ended questions that give our client space to talk and share valuable information that we may not have even thought to ask. This also gives us plenty of new information to ask follow-up questions, that make it feel more like a conversation than a business consultation.

Open-ended questions usually start with who, what, when, where, or why. For example, instead of asking, "Do you want service 'x' or service 'y'?" ask, "What type of service are you looking for?"

Observe people while listening to them—truly look at them. Get curious and become comfortable with silence. The less you talk, the more you'll learn about them. Make it about them not about you. Be prepared with questions that interest you but allow the conversation to stray from your plan to what interests *them*.

According to a study reported in the *Journal of Social and Personal Relationship*, it takes approximately 50 hours of time together to move from acquaintance to casual friend, 90 hours to become a friend and more than 200 hours before you can consider someone a close friend. Keep this in mind when establishing a business relationship with a client.

Relationships take time.

The sweetest thing you can say is someone's name

A name is a connection to one's identity. Remembering someone's name is one of the quickest ways to build rapport with them. We feel important and validated when a person refers to us by name during a conversation. Because it's rare when people remember our name after initially meeting us, it makes us feel connected to someone when they do remember.

Be specific with compliments

Another way we feel seen is when someone shows appreciation for us. A meaningful compliment can go a long way in establishing connection with another. Sharing our appreciation for someone, needs to be specific to make them feel seen. The more specific the better. Saying, "I appreciate you" is not as powerful as saying, "I appreciate how kind you are to others."

What drives your business?

In his book, *Start With Why*, Simon Sinek writes, "People don't buy what you do; they buy why you do it. And what you do simply proves what you believe." People are attracted to businesses that make them feel special, like they belong to something important. Our potential clients already know what we do. But to stand out from other similar businesses we need to be clear about *why* we do what we do. For example, in Sinek's book, he shares a story about the introduction of the Apple iPod. At the time, there was already a similar technology available. The difference was the competing company advertised their product as a "5GB mp3 player" and Apple advertised the iPod as "1,000 songs in your pocket." The competition told us *what* their product was, and Apple told us *why* we needed it.

When we have a clear sense of why we offer the product or service that we offer (not just to make money), we don't have to convince anyone of our value and don't have to be obsessed with what the competition is doing. Because we're different, those we encounter will know it by our words and actions.

Decisions are primarily emotionally driven. We don't buy products and services only because we need them. We buy them because of how they make us feel. Because of who is selling them and what they represent to us. We crave connection and purpose above all else and no list of benefits and features can compare to the power of a purpose that resonates with clients.

Magnanimous people genuinely care about connecting with others and providing value.

When people associate us with positive memories, good feelings, and meaningful purposes, they're far more likely to do business with us. Connecting with our clients is the fastest and most enduring way to attract and keep clients for years to come.

#4

making good decisions

Life's greatest gift is choice. Choice is the ability to select one course of action over others to direct our experience. Whether you hate your job, are unhappy in a relationship, or long to travel the world, the choices you make will either take you closer to fulfillment or farther away from it.

Decisions cause mental fatigue

According to a study on mindless eating (Wansink and Sobal, 2007), we make over 200 decisions about food alone each day. In an article published in the *Wall Street Journal,* the author speculates that we may possibly make "35,000 remotely conscious decisions per day."

That's a lot of decisions.

It's no wonder by the end of the day the last thing we want to do is make another decision, even choosing something as simple as what to eat for dinner.

Making decisions causes mental fatigue. The more choices we make throughout the day, the more our brain struggles with decisions, and it eventually begins to look for shortcuts. Without a mental break, this can cause us to choose impulsively or to do nothing due to exhaustion. This is why we make better decisions in the morning and are more susceptible to bad decisions (eating ice cream for dinner) later in the day.

Apple cofounder Steve Jobs wore the same outfit every day, which preserved his energy for more significant decision-making.

We could follow Jobs' example with our own daily decisions. I will go to the gym Tuesday and Thursday. I will not have more than two cups of coffee. I will prepare my clothes for tomorrow before I go to bed.

When possible, we can eliminate the need for everyday decisions and save our energy for more important decisions by establishing rules for ourselves.

Too many choices can overwhelm

When making a decision, the more options we have, the more prone we are to make regrettable decisions due to "choice paralysis." To avoid this, we can minimize the number of options for consideration by reducing our must-have criteria. Then, once we've found a solution that meets our needs, we stop searching.

The same goes for our clients. We can help prevent their indecision by asking questions that help us narrow their options for them. Then, they can make a good enough decision rather than stay stuck in trying to make the perfect decision.

I enjoy encouraging new writers to write and contribute their unique voices to the world. I have encountered many writers who have been writing the same book for decades, but never published because it's still not perfect. The truth is, it will never be perfect. If they're learning and growing, there will always be something to improve. When a writer shoots for "good enough" instead of "perfect," they can finish their work and move on to the next project.

There are no perfect solutions. Instead of wasting valuable time and energy searching for perfection, potentially leaving us with little or no time to make a good decision, we can make *good enough* decisions.

Make *good enough* decisions

The author of *Paradox of Choice: Why Less is More*, psychologist Barry Schwartz, argues that people who spend the most time and energy obsessing over making *exactly the right choice* end up less happy with their decisions than the people who make a choice that's *good enough*.

In choosing good enough, we aren't saying we don't care about the choices we're making. Instead, we've limited our criteria to what's most important, and once our criteria are met, we make our decision quickly and move on with our lives.

People who settle for *good enough* are consistently happier than people who must choose the best possible option. Seeking perfection can also lead to indecision. Good enough is almost always good enough. If it doesn't work out, we can simply make another *good enough* decision.

Failure is a beautiful necessity

When we make decisions, we're motivated not only by the opportunity for gain, but also by fear. Fear of making a mistake. Fear of failure. These fears can keep us stuck.

Scientists fail every day. Failure is an essential part of scientific research. Setbacks don't have to be the end of the story. A setback might be exactly what we need to get to where we want to be.

Walt Disney was no stranger to failure.

Early in his career he lost creative control of his first character, Oswald the Rabbit. Later, his Mickey Mouse character was rejected by the studio because they believed women were afraid of mice. And lastly, before the screening of *Pinocchio*, Disney hired several people to stand on top of the marquee, dressed as Pinocchio, and wave at the families coming into the theater. He provided them with food and wine for the day. By the time the screening began, the Pinocchios were drunk, naked, and swearing at the crowd.

These are just a few of the many *failures* Disney experienced in his career, but these setbacks didn't dull his imagination or deter him from going on to innovate technologies and create the Disney empire, which is worth $167 billion today.

Failure is part of life and with proper perspective can be seen as a beautiful necessity. How many times did we have to stumble and fall before learning how to walk? What if after the first couple of failed attempts we'd simply given up? We'd still be crawling instead of walking. Great innovation and proficiency are often the result of trial and error.

We can train ourselves to be comfortable with discomfort by looking for small challenges we can take on where the stakes for failure are low. The more we practice this, the less scary failure becomes.

Taking our power back

In the book, *Man's Search for Meaning*, neurologist and Holocaust survivor Viktor Frankl wrote, "We are self-determining. What we become—within the limits of endowment and environment—we've made out of ourselves. In the concentration camps, for example, in this living laboratory and on this testing ground, we watched and witnessed some of our comrades behave like swine while others behaved like saints. **Man has both potentialities within himself; which one is actualized depends on *decisions* but not on conditions.**"

We always have a choice. Even in a concentration camp we can choose *how to respond* to our circumstances.

Psychologist Marsha Linehan, who created *dialectic behavior therapy*, teaches *radical acceptance*. Radical acceptance means that we acknowledge what IS rather than fight or reject reality and at the same time figure out what to do about it to make the situation better—not by changing other people, but by changing what *we* are thinking and doing.

Sometimes we may not like our current options, but that doesn't mean we don't have a choice. It simply means we don't see a good choice. Choosing to do nothing is also a choice.

There is great power in acknowledging our choice, especially when we feel stuck without good options. We can acknowledge, "I choose this." I choose to stay at this job I hate. I choose to stay in this unhappy relationship. I choose to put off traveling the world. We may have good reasons for choosing to stay at a job we hate, but denying our choice makes us victims. As long as we stay stuck in "Why is this happening to me?" or "I have no choice" we give away our power. When we take ownership of our choice and say, "I choose this," it empowers us to make a different choice.

Our choices demonstrate our priorities

Many of us live a life of busyness. Wake up, rush from one task to the next, crash into bed unable to sleep as our minds race with the next day's tasks. Repeat.

We stay busy to the point of distraction. We have a list of things we *would* do if *only we had more time*—work out, take up a hobby, eat healthier, etc. We are so busy and distracted that not only are we not living our dreams, we've completely forgotten them.

Let's get honest about our priorities. A friend told me that he wanted to eat healthier, but his work schedule was so crazy that he just didn't have time to plan healthy meals and was too exhausted at the end of the day to prepare anything. In other words, he didn't have *time* to eat healthier. During the pandemic, he worked from home and had plenty of time to eat healthier. Yet, he still didn't. Why not?

Because the truth is our actions have always demonstrated our priorities. We didn't do those things previously because they weren't truly a priority. We *make* time for what is important to us. This realization is a good thing because now we can ask ourselves honestly "What *is* important to me?"

Our most powerful tool for navigating our circumstances is choice. The decisions we make have the potential to positively contribute to our wellbeing, carve out our experiences, and move us closer to the realization of our goals.

We can make *choices* going forward that manifest a more meaningful and rewarding life.

Choice can also dictate how we are perceived by our clients.

Magnanimous people understand that good decision-making instills confidence in those around us and assures them that we're capable of meeting their needs.

Making sure our actions match our stated priorities promotes trust with our clients. If we say, "I'm sorry I haven't gotten back to you, I've been really busy" to a client or potential client, what we're really communicating is "You are not a priority."

"Choice transforms us into artists. Each of us becomes another Michelangelo, for choice is the chisel we use to sculpt our life." – *Gary McGuire*

We hold the chisel for our life. Choice by choice, we can sculpt an abundant future.

Use your intuition for better decision-making

Intuition is a sense of knowing without knowing how we know. Sometimes called gut instinct, a hunch, or a deeper knowing, this describes our ability to know something without conscious reasoning—solutions come to us but we aren't exactly sure how or why.

Science calls the gut our *second* brain. While this brain is primarily responsible for the function of digestion, it also communicates with the brain in our skull. Scientists know that our thoughts affect our mood, but recent studies show that our gut brain also affects our wellbeing.

Our gut is smart and knows what we need to do. It transmits that knowledge to the skull brain as a *feeling*. The skull brain then tries to make sense of that feeling. Often this shows up as an urge to do something or not do something, but we can't seem to articulate the reasons, so we doubt ourselves.

Studies show that combining gut feelings with analytical thinking helps us make quicker, more accurate decisions. Even the U.S. Navy has invested millions of dollars into training sailors and Marines to develop their intuition for quick life-or-death decision-making on the battlefield. [7]

We can use our intuition to make the best decisions in business.

Recognizing and accessing intuition

When we feel uneasy about something, rather than rationalize it away, we can pay attention to the discomfort we're experiencing. We can ask questions that help us gain clarity. For example, if we're feeling uneasy about meeting with someone, we can ask ourselves, "Do I want to meet with this person?" If the answer is "yes" and we feel relaxed about our response, we can ask follow-up questions to identify where the uneasiness is coming from. If we then ask, "Do I want to drive for three hours to meet them?" and the answer is "no," maybe our unease means we want to meet them, but at a different location. We can follow this line of questioning any time we feel uneasy about a situation or decision, until we identify the solution that makes our body feel relaxed.

The biggest hinderance to using our intuition is our need to articulate why a choice makes us uneasy. Sometimes our questions are left unanswered. We simply don't know "why." When this happens, we often discount our intuition and make the choice that "makes sense." *Ignoring* our intuition can lead to results that have us asking why we didn't trust our gut. *Paying attention* to our intuition can lead to results that are beyond our wildest dreams.

At the end of 2010, I was the director of several technology departments for an insurance company. I had been in tech for thirty years and management for eight years. I was burnt out. I wanted to do something different but couldn't see the path out. It was budget time and we needed to cut a substantial dollar amount from the tech budget to offset company losses. I knew the largest dollars are always realized from eliminating salaries. I also knew that we were already running leaner than we should be and couldn't afford to let anyone go. As I sat across from the chief information officer, discussing the potential elimination of specific software, I got a little nudge from my intuition. It said, "You can eliminate you."

What? My boss continued to talk, and I explored this thought further. The other directors could easily absorb my three departments, thus eliminating the need for my position, and realizing an immediate savings of $120,000. At that point I hadn't thought through the details, but the idea gave me an overwhelming sense of peace.

I decided to trust my gut and shared this idea with my boss, who was unsurprisingly shocked. A week later at our next meeting I proposed an exit strategy that allowed me time to transition my teams and a compensation package that would allow me time to figure out my next move.

I was stepping into the unknown and was both a little frightened and more at peace than I'd been in a long time. I went on to explore a childhood dream of writing a book. I had no idea what steps were needed to accomplish this dream, but I focused on one step at a time, trusting my intuition along the way. Two years later my first nonfiction book reached bestseller status and is still my bestselling book today.

Our body is the best barometer of what's right for us. When we make a choice using our intuition, we will experience peace, a *knowing* that it is right. This doesn't mean the choice is always easy, but when it's right, it will bring us a sense of peace about our decision.

The science behind intuition suggests that this may be a superpower we want to develop to give us an advantage in business.

Magnanimous people take advantage of this superpower.

#5

harness imagination for creative solutions

Psychology experts tell us that children spend as much as 67% of their time in non-reality—in their imagination—and that this is a critical aspect of our development. As we mature into adulthood and beyond, we're confronted with practicality, responsibility, and survival. We shift from seeing the refrigerator box as a potential fort to seeing it as a cardboard box. Our imagination is not gone, we simply use it less. A lot less. But we still use it.

94 | mag.nan.i.mous

Imagination helps us explore possibilities

When we replay a conversation in our head, the one where we wish we'd said something different, we're using our imaginations. When we practice asking our boss for a raise, we're using our imaginations. When we are in the shower and suddenly have a great idea, that's our imagination at work.

Imagination is the ability to create visual images in our minds, the place where we can explore ideas, scenarios, conversations, and our ideal lives without the constraints of the physical world.

This imagining helps us come up with alternative ways of seeing an issue and alternative ways of being in the world. In our thoughts there are no limits, failures, or consequences, so we can freely fantasize.

As children we dreamed of what we wanted to be when we grew up. As adults we can dream of a new future.

Constraints make us more creative

Constraints force us to think more creatively. When we limit our options, we push our minds to invent new ideas and solutions. For example, if we're given a blank sheet of paper and asked to write a story, we may become paralyzed by choice. Too many options and no idea where to begin. But if we're asked to write a story using exactly six words, our choices are immediately narrowed to something manageable which frees us to explore unfamiliar solutions.

A popular example of this six-word assignment (author unknown) is profound: "For Sale: Baby shoes. Never worn."

Obstacles boost brain power. "Creative constraints" are used by most product development departments. They force us to think "outside the box" and according to psychologists, when we have less to work with, we begin to see the world differently.

The "Nursery Without Toys" experiment conducted over twenty years ago in Germany removed all toys from their kindergarten classrooms for three months and gave children the freedom (with adult supervision) to do what they wanted, however they wanted. Because they were not being directed by the teachers, they had to find new ways to occupy their day.

On the first day, the children were confused and bored. By the second day, the kids were playing with chairs and blankets, making forts by draping blankets over tables and weighing them down with shoes. Shortly thereafter they were running around, chatting and laughing excitedly. By the end of the third month, they were engaged in outrageously imaginative play, able to concentrate better and communicate more effectively.

Fewer options allow space to nurture our creativity, problem-solving abilities, and social skills.

Exercise fuels imagination

A study on creative thinking published by the American Psychological Association in 2014 found that walking substantially enhances creativity and increases appropriate novel idea generation. On average, researchers observed a 60% increase in creative output from participants both while walking as well as when they sat down to do creative work shortly after a walk. [8]

Going for a walk not only unlocks rut-like thinking, it gives us access to fresh ideas.

Imagining a new future

If we've ever thought about buying a new car, we've experienced what happens when we get clear about what we want. We decide to buy a new Toyota Rav4 and now everywhere we go, we see this make and model of car. But it's not that everyone had the same idea and bought the same car, it's that our brains are now aware of them because of our intention to own one.

By using our imaginations to dream, we can get clear about what we want in our lives. Once we have clarity, we will naturally become aware of things that will help us realize those dreams that we previously weren't aware of. Our logical and imaginative minds work in collaboration.

Here's an imagination exercise to get you started:

1. Select an area of your business where you're dissatisfied or have an unfulfilled dream.
2. Focus on that one area or dream, imagine yourself at a future date, in your ideal scenario, one to three years from now in as much detail as possible.
3. Where are you? At your home? At a new home? On the beach? In a restaurant? What are you doing? Are you with someone? Are you alone?
4. Create a scene in your mind of yourself living out your ideal life. How do you feel? Visualize all the details,

feel all the sensations. Imagine you are truly there, living that life.

When we allow ourselves the luxury of creating and experiencing our ideal lives in our minds, we provide not only a space of blissful entertainment, but we could be laying the foundation for a new reality.

#6

be true to yourself

Negotiation is not the same as compromise. In negotiation, we each get something we want in exchange for giving up something. In compromise, we meet somewhere in the middle and neither of us gets what we truly want—we sell out to achieve some short-term goal while ignoring our core values and beliefs.

Don't compromise who you are

Every time we compromise on something that is vital to who we are, we deny our authentic selves. The farther we move away from who we are, the more unhappy we become. Whether it's to please others or to prevent "rocking the boat," if we ignore what we need, our abandonment leaves us unfulfilled. This eventually creates resentment and is poisonous not only to our happiness, but to our relationships.

**"Tolerance is the virtue of the man
without convictions."**
– G.K. Chesterton

It's okay to have convictions, even in business. The number one regret of the dying is "I wish I'd had the courage to live a life true to myself, not the life others expected of me."

Many of us spend a great deal of time trying to be something we're not. We have our reasons—to fit in, to build business relationships, to win friends and influence people, to avoid scrutiny ... But the quickest path to true success is to quit focusing on how others see us and get comfortable with who we are.

When we share our story honestly, when we share our genuine selves, we not only let our confidence shine, we empower others to do likewise. Authenticity is transformative.

Putting ourselves out there, no matter how vulnerable it feels, is the only real way to truly *be* ourselves.

In Maslow's hierarchy of needs, self-actualization is the highest level of psychological development, where personal potential is fully realized after basic bodily and ego needs have been fulfilled. The self-actualized are autonomous—not dependent on other people or culture, for their satisfaction and growth.

They know who they are, and they aren't seeking other people's approval.

**"If you've gotta think about being cool,
you ain't cool."**
– Keith Richards

True self-acceptance means we present to the world all our glorious uncool qualities. Because that is who we authentically are.

Clinical psychologist Dr. Julie Gurner says, "A cool person is someone whose attitude and behaviors are composed but seen as uniquely their own. People are genuinely drawn to cool people because they see them as a representation of who they wish to be — confident in who they are."

Magnanimous people are cool.

It's exhausting trying to be something we aren't anyway. Let's embrace our magnificent imperfection, be uniquely who we are, and attract the clients we actually *want* to do business with.

#7

it's all about people

Ultimately, in business and in life, it's all about relationships with people. The better we get at genuinely caring about others, the more attractive we become. The more attractive we become, the more people want to do business with us. But we must start with ourselves. If we don't truly care about ourselves, we can't truly care about others either—and they'll know it.

Conclusion

Magnanimous people accept and even appreciate their imperfections, which gives them the ability to more easily accept the imperfections of others. They recognize their unique creative and humanitarian potential—how they add value to the world.

Magnanimous people look for opportunities to add value, because they understand that when we add value, everyone benefits. Whether it's genuinely listening to someone or providing a creative solution to a client's problem, they know that every time they contribute their great-hearted talent and skills to the world, they are attracting more goodness into their own lives.

Including all the business they could ever want.

"I have found that if you love life, life will love you back."
-Arthur Rubenstein

notes

[1] Karen Wynn, "The moral baby (2014)" https://psycnet.apa.org/record/2013-21910-020 (last accessed 22 November 2023)

[2] Stephanie Brown, "Providing social support may be more beneficial than receiving it: results from a prospective study of mortality (2003)" https://pubmed.ncbi.nlm.nih.gov/12807404/ (last accessed 22 November 2023)

[3] Dorian Peters, Rafael Calvo, "Compassion vs. empathy: designing for resilience (2014)" https://dl.acm.org/doi/fullHtml/10.1145/2647087 (last accessed 22 November 2023).

[4] Michal Kosinski, "Frankly, We Do Give a Damn: The Relationship Between Profanity and Honesty (2017)" https://www.gsb.stanford.edu/faculty-research/publications/frankly-we-do-give-damn-relationship-between-profanity-honesty (last accessed 22 November 2023)

[5] Michal Kosinski, "Frankly, We Do Give a Damn: The Relationship Between Profanity and Honesty (2017)" https://journals.sagepub.com/doi/full/10.1177/1948550616681055 (last accessed 22 November 2023)

6   Leanne ten Brinke, "Some Evidence for Unconscious Lie Detection (2014)" http://www.leannetenbrinke.com/uploads/2/1/0/4/21049652/ten _brinke_stimson___carney_2014.pdf (last accessed 22 November 2023)

7   Galang Lufityanto, "Measuring Intuition: Nonconscious Emotional Information Boosts Decision Accuracy and Confidence (2016)" http://www.leannetenbrinke.com/uploads/2/1/0/4/21049652/ten _brinke_stimson___carney_2014.pdf (last accessed 22 November 2023)

8   Marily Oppezzo, "Give Your Ideas Some Legs: The Positive Effect of Walking on Creative Thinking (2014)" https://www.apa.org/pubs/journals/releases/xlm-a0036577.pdf (last accessed 22 November 2023)

about the author

DAYNA JO MASON

Born and raised in Seattle, Washington, by her single mom on public assistance, Dayna was driven to entrepreneurship at an early age.

As a 9-year-old, when she wasn't eavesdropping on her mom's conversations with troubled friends and writing down her thoughts, she was making money—everything from selling her drawings on the street corner, to knocking on neighbors' doors and offering to sweep driveways or sell them flowers (picked in the neighborhood).

Dayna has enjoyed a thirty-year career in technology, working for Bank of America, Boeing, and lastly serving as a technology director for a regional insurance company. She's owned and operated several successful businesses in the fields of wedding ministry, writing, book publishing, and real estate investing and consulting.

Dayna has always been fascinated by what makes people tick and felt great compassion for the human struggle. She's written dozens of articles and books to create awareness of options for overcoming challenges and realizing lasting health and happiness. Her lifelong commitment to inspiring people to make meaningful changes in their lives drives her every day.

She is currently enjoying life in Southern California as a grandma, real estate consultant, and inspirational author.

Other Books by Dayna Mason (Reid)

Books by Dayna Mason

"**Dayna's Dose:** A Prescription of Articles to Enrich Your Life"

"**Mosley the Feelings Monster**" (a children's book)

"**Women Over 50 the A to Z of It**" (a colorful book filled with inspirational messages)

Books by Dayna Reid

"**Do-It-Yourself Wedding Ceremony** *Guidebook*: Choosing the Perfect Words and Officiating Your Unforgettable Day"

"**Funerals & Memorials:** Creating the Perfect Service to Remember a Loved One"

"**Officiating Weddings:** Start a Profitable Business Marrying Couples"

"**Wedding Officiant Guidebook For Beginners:** How to Become Ordained and Perform a Marriage Ceremony Script"

Hi Reader!

I hope you've enjoyed this book and found the information valuable, maybe even life changing. Thank you for taking the time to read it. I love hearing from my readers, so please feel free to reach out and let me know your thoughts or share your own stories.

If you feel moved to do so, I'd love it if you would post a review on Amazon, **Barnes** & Noble, or wherever you shop online for books. ☺

I look forward to connecting with you!

Thank you!

Dayna

Connect with me:

www.daynajo.com

Made in United States
North Haven, CT
05 July 2024

54415322R00068